ENTERPRISE

CLAY

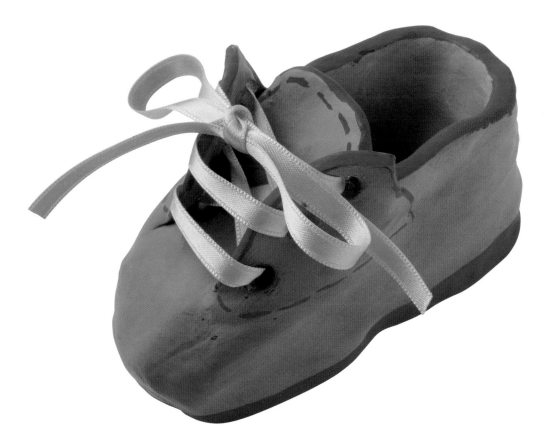

Gareth Stevens Publishing
A WORLD ALMANAC EDUCATION GROUP COMPANY

Please visit our web site at: www.garethstevens.com
For a free color catalog describing Gareth Stevens Publishing's
list of high-quality books and multimedia programs,
call 1-800-542-2595 (USA) or 1-800-387-3178 (Canada).
Gareth Stevens Publishing's fax: (414) 332-3567.

Library of Congress Cataloging-in-Publication Data

Clay.
      p. cm. — (Let's create!)
    Summary: Step-by-step instructions show how to use different types
of clay and acrylic paints to create original craft projects.
    Includes bibliographical references.
    ISBN 0-8368-3746-0 (lib. bdg.)
    1. Pottery craft—Juvenile literature.   2. Clay—Juvenile literature.
[1. Pottery craft. 2. Clay. 3. Handicraft.] I. Series.
TT920.C59   2003
738—dc21   2003045406

This North American edition first published in 2003 by
Gareth Stevens Publishing
A World Almanac Education Group Company
330 West Olive Street, Suite 100
Milwaukee, WI 53212 USA

First published as *¡Vamos a crear! Barro* with an original copyright © 2001 by
Parramón Ediciones, S.A., – World Rights, text and illustrations by Parramón's
Editorial Team. This U.S. edition copyright © 2004 by Gareth Stevens, Inc.
Additional end matter copyright © 2004 by Gareth Stevens, Inc.

English Translation: Colleen Coffey
Gareth Stevens Series Editor: Dorothy L. Gibbs
Gareth Stevens Designer: Katherine A. Goedheer

Printed in Spain

1 2 3 4 5 6 7 8 9 07 06 05 04 03

Table of Contents

Introduction

Clay is a material that can easily be shaped into many different objects. This book offers a dozen ideas for craft projects made of clay. The projects are fun to do, and the objects are both decorative and useful.

For the projects in this book, you will need only a few basic tools for shaping clay: a spatula, a wire sculpting loop, a plastic knife, and your hands.

Each project shows you how to work with clay in a different way. For the Hat 'n' Scarf Doll, you start by making sausage shapes. For the Cutout Candleholder, you flatten clay with a rolling pin. For other projects, shapes are molded, carved, or even cut out with cookie cutters. You will learn several different techniques and see interesting results.

Clay comes in many different types, colors, and textures. The projects in this book are made with self-hardening clay, which is a type of clay that hardens by air-drying. Self-hardening clay does not have to be baked in an oven. All of the projects use brown clay or white clay. For some projects, you will be told to use both colors to get the best results. Remember that brown clay is messier to use because it can stain hands, clothing, and other materials.

All of the projects are painted with acrylic paints. In some cases, however, parts of a project are left unpainted to show the original color of the clay. Keep in mind that any clay object can be varnished after the clay has hardened. Varnish makes a clay object stronger and not as easy to damage.

Watch for special instructions at the end of each project to try other great ideas. Sometimes, making just one small change creates a very different result.

Get ready to play and have fun with clay!

5

Hat 'n' Scarf Doll

You can make this well-dressed doll with only two pieces of clay! Just follow six easy steps.

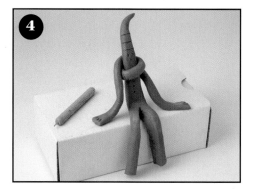

1 Roll two pieces of brown clay into sausage shapes. Make one sausage thinner than the other. The thick sausage will be the doll's body. Roll one end of the thick sausage into a point. The pointed end forms the doll's hat.

2 To form the doll's legs, use a plastic knife to cut the thick sausage in half from about the middle of it to the end that is not pointed.

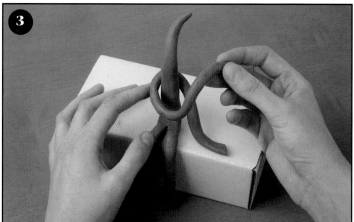

3 Bend the clay body to make the doll sit on the edge of the small cardboard box. Wrap the thin clay sausage around the top of the body like a scarf. The ends of the scarf are the doll's arms, and they help balance the doll on the box.

You will need:
- brown clay
- plastic knife
- small cardboard box
- pick
- green, blue, and yellow paints
- paintbrush

4 With a pick or the point of a sharp pencil, make dots and lines in the clay for fingers, eyes, buttons, and stripes on the hat.

5 When the clay is dry and has hardened, separate the two sausage shapes so they will be easier to paint. Paint the doll's body and legs green and decorate its hat with blue and yellow stripes.

6 Paint the scarf (arms) blue. Then decorate the scarf by painting green and yellow polka dots on it.

Now your doll is all dressed up and ready to decorate a tabletop or a bookshelf.

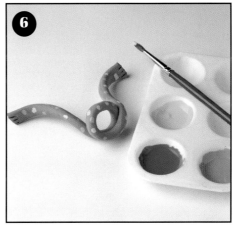

Another Great Idea!
Bend the doll's body and its scarf to form a different pose. You can make a whole collection of different poses!

Cutout Candleholder

With a small piece of clay and a rolling pin, you can make this clever candleholder. Cutout shapes in the sides let the candlelight flicker through.

You will need:
- white clay
- rolling pin
- plastic knife
- tooth-edged spatula
- blue and yellow paints
- paintbrushes
- toothbrush

1 Flatten a piece of white clay with a rolling pin and cut it into a rectangle with a plastic knife. Then cut a curvy line along one of the two long sides of the rectangle.

2 With the tip of the plastic knife, draw small geometric shapes all over the rectangle. Then use the plastic knife to carve out all the different shapes and remove them.

3 With a tooth-edged spatula, make little marks along one short side of the rectangle. Bring the short sides around to touch each other and press the clay together to form a cylinder. Wet your fingertip with water to smooth out the seam.

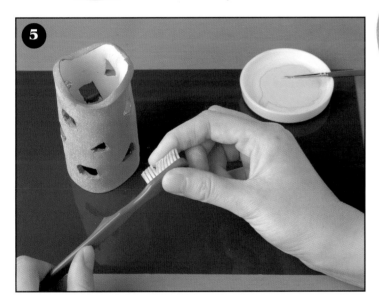

④ When the clay is dry and has hardened, paint the outside of the cylinder blue.

⑤ When the blue paint is dry, dip a toothbrush into yellow paint and carefully spatter the paint onto the cylinder to decorate it.

Another Great Idea!
Model a round, flat piece of clay that you can use as a plate under your fantastic candleholder.

Put a small candle into this decorative holder and ask a grown-up to light the candle for you. Then turn off all the lights and enjoy the candle's glow.

9

Treasure Shoe

One . . . two . . . model a shoe. Three . . . four . . . use it to store treasures, trinkets — and more!

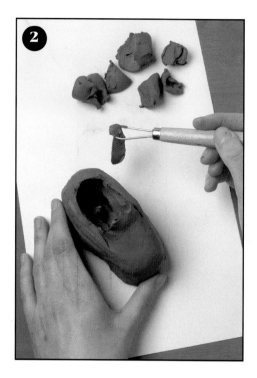

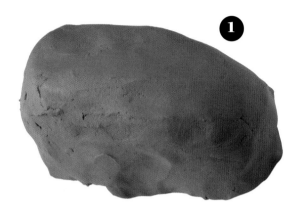

1 Use your hands to model a lump of brown clay into the shape of a shoe.

2 Use a wire sculpting loop to remove clay from the inside of the shoe, but leave a tongue of clay on the shoe.

3 Flatten another piece of clay with a rolling pin. Use a pick to draw two side flaps for the shoe into the flat piece of clay. Cut out the side flaps with a plastic knife. Use the eraser end of a pencil to make three holes along the curve of each side flap.

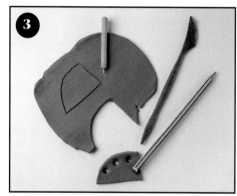

You will need:
- brown clay
- wire sculpting loop
- rolling pin
- pick
- plastic knife
- pencil
- green and red paints
- paintbrush
- yellow ribbon

4 Attach the side flaps to the shoe. Press one flap on each side of the tongue and smooth the pieces of clay together with your fingers.

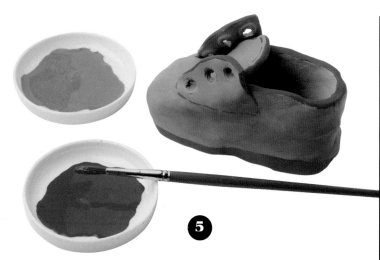 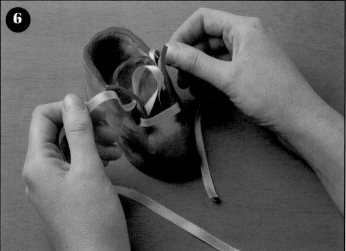

5 When the clay is dry and has hardened, paint the shoe green. When the green paint is dry, decorate the edges of the sole and the shoe opening with red paint. Use red paint to add stitching, too.

6 Thread a piece of yellow ribbon through the holes in the side flaps, the same way you lace a shoe. Tie the ribbon into a bow.

Now... don't you agree that modeling a shoe is as easy as 1, 2, 3? Just add treasures!

Another Great Idea!
Use a real shoelace, instead of ribbon, to tie the shoe. You can also make another style of shoe. How about clogs?

Paper Clip Plate

Turn a pretty painted plate into a person to protect your paper clips.

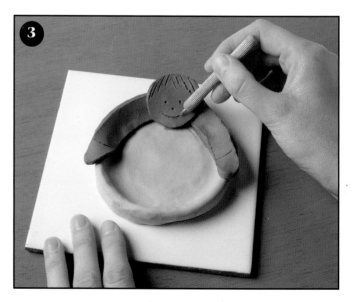

1 Use your hands to model a ball of white clay into a flat circle. Roll another piece of clay into a thin sausage shape and press it around the edge of the circle to form a raised border.

2 Flatten a piece of brown clay with a rolling pin. Use a pick to draw a circle for a face and two long rectangles for arms. Cut out all three shapes with a plastic knife.

You will need:
- white clay
- brown clay
- rolling pin
- pick
- plastic knife
- yellow and blue paints
- paintbrush

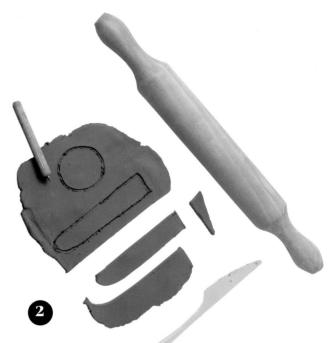

3 Attach the face and arm shapes to the raised edge of the plate. Use the pick to draw hands and the features of the face.

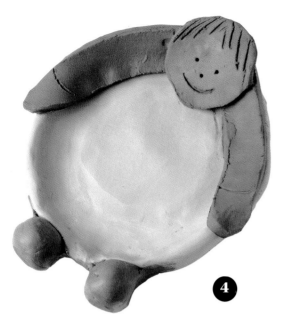

4

4 To add shoes, roll two small balls of brown clay. Attach them to the edge of the plate, straight across from the face. Smooth the clay with your fingers to blend the tops of the balls into the edge of the plate.

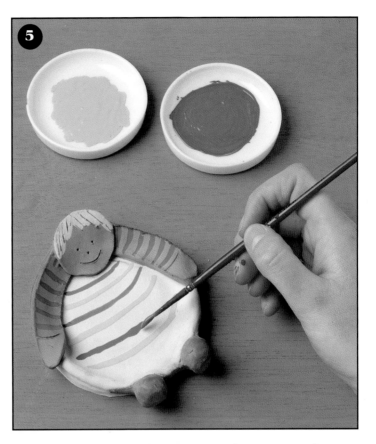

5

5 Paint your plate person's hair yellow. Then paint blue stripes on the arms and yellow and blue stripes across the body.

This cheerful plate person will take care of paper clips or any other small objects that need protecting.

Another Great Idea!
Use the same color of clay to model both the plate and the person, then paint them both with bright color combinations.

Quick-Change Clown

Geometric clay shapes can stack up to be a clever and changeable clay clown — or any other character you care to create.

You will need:
- brown clay
- wooden skewers
- different colored paints
- paintbrushes
- white clay

1 Use your hands to model a piece of brown clay into a thick triangle shape. Poke a wooden skewer into the center of the triangle.

2 When the clay triangle is dry and has hardened, paint it orange.

3 Roll pieces of clay between the palms of your hands to make balls of both brown and white clay. Use a wooden skewer to poke a hole through each ball.

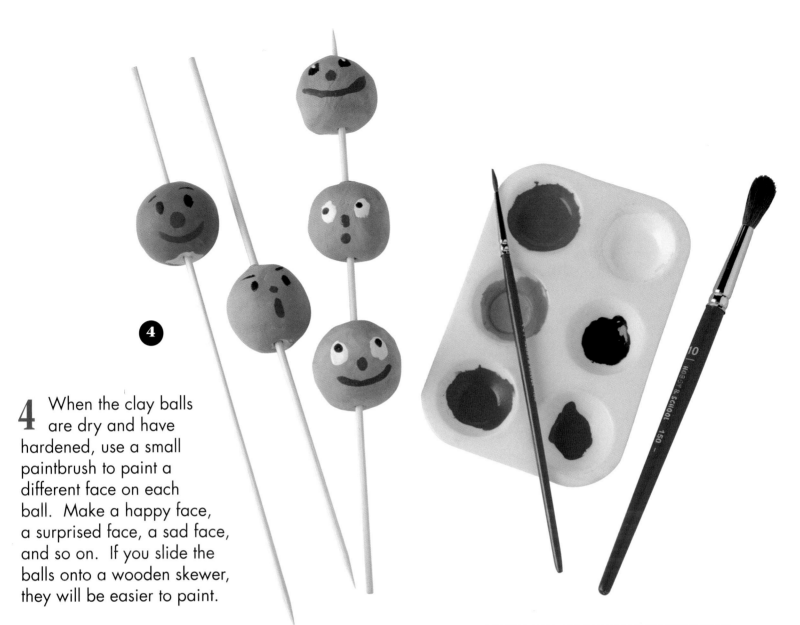

4 When the clay balls are dry and have hardened, use a small paintbrush to paint a different face on each ball. Make a happy face, a surprised face, a sad face, and so on. If you slide the balls onto a wooden skewer, they will be easier to paint.

5 Model square and rectangle shapes by gently hitting lumps of clay against a hard surface. Try to make all of the shapes about the same thickness. Poke a hole through each of the shapes with a wooden skewer.

6 When the clay squares and rectangles are dry and have hardened, paint each of them a different color. Let the first coat of paint dry, then paint on designs, such as stripes or polka dots, in contrasting colors.

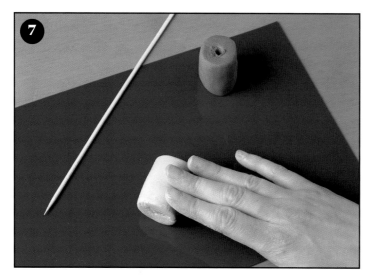

7 Roll lumps of clay into thick cylinder shapes. Flatten the ends by hitting them gently against a hard surface. Make a hole through the center of each cylinder.

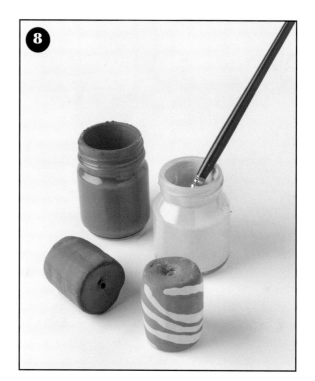

8 When the clay cylinders are dry and have hardened, paint and decorate each one differently.

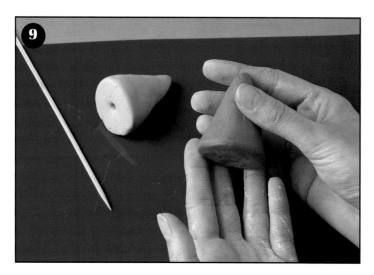

9 Roll and model lumps of clay with your hands to make cone shapes of both brown and white clay. Flatten the bottom of each cone by hitting it gently against a hard surface. Poke a wooden skewer into the bottom of each cone. Push the skewer only halfway into the shape. The hole should not go all the way through the cone.

10 When the cone shapes are dry and have hardened, paint each cone any color you like, then decorate each cone with fancy painted designs in many bright colors.

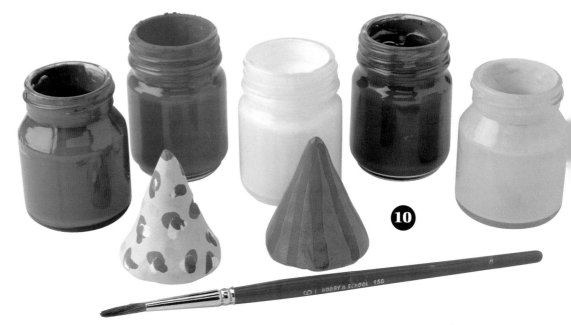

11 Now you can put your clown together. Slide any combination of squares, rectangles, and cylinders onto the skewer that is stuck in the clay triangle. Leave enough room at the top of the skewer to slide on one ball, for a head, and one cone, for a hat.

A handful of geometric shapes, stacked in all kinds of different ways, will create dozens of clever clay clowns.

Another Great Idea!
Make as many geometric shapes as you want and combine them in as many different ways as you can think of. Varnish the pieces to make them stronger.

Whale Safe

To keep a lid on small secrets, put them inside this crafty clay whale.

You will need:
- brown clay
- fishing line or thick nylon thread
- wire sculpting loop
- blue, black, and white paints
- paintbrushes

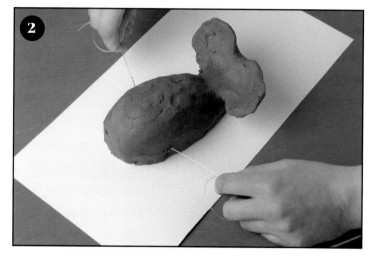

1 Use your hands to model a large lump of brown clay into the body of a whale with a very big tail.

2 Use a piece of fishing line or thick nylon thread to cut the whale in half from its head to its tail. The bottom half will be the base of the whale. The top half will be the lid.

3 Roll a piece of clay into a thick sausage shape. Attach it to the lid, around the inside edge, by pressing and smoothing the clay with your fingers. This ridge will keep the lid from sliding off the base.

4 Use a wire loop to take clay out of the base of the whale. Be careful not to make any holes in the bottom or the sides of the base.

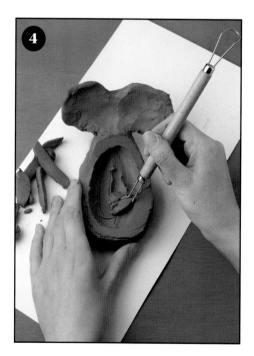

5 Roll another thick sausage shape and split it halfway down to make a handle that looks like a spray of water. Attach the handle to the whale's lid by pressing and smoothing the clay with your fingers.

18

6 When your clay whale is dry and has hardened, paint the handle blue, the eyes black, and the mouth white. Paint black lines on the mouth to make teeth. Then paint with blue and white around the bottom of the base and the ends of the tail to look like ocean waves.

Keep valuables undercover inside your whale for safekeeping.

Another Great Idea!
Model a turtle or a crab — or both! Cut the clay in half so the shell becomes the lid of the box.

Clay Mobile

Clay cutouts on pieces of cord or string are the key ingredients for creating a decorative mobile to dangle from the ceiling.

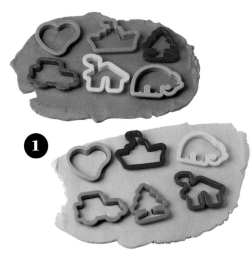

1 Flatten pieces of brown and white clay with a rolling pin. Place cookie cutters of different shapes and sizes on top of the clay. Press each cookie cutter down hard enough to cut through the clay.

2 Lift the cookie cutters off the clay and remove the cutouts. Use a toothpick to make a small hole at the top of each cutout.

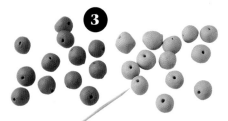

3 With the clay left over from the cutouts, make small clay balls. Use a toothpick to poke holes through the balls.

You will need:
- brown clay
- white clay
- rolling pin
- cookie cutters
- toothpicks
- different colored paints
- paintbrush
- scissors
- cord or string
- thin wooden dowels

4 When all of the clay shapes and balls are dry and have hardened, paint them with different colors and designs.

5 Cut six pieces of cord or string. Tie clay shapes and string balls, in different combinations, onto each piece of cord. Try to make each combination about the same size.

6 Arrange three wooden dowels in a star pattern and tie them together in the middle. Tie each piece of cord to the end of a dowel.

With just a gentle tap or a soft breeze, the cutouts on your clay mobile will start a whirling, twirling dance high overhead.

Another Great Idea!
Don't use cookie cutters to make the clay shapes for your mobile. Model shapes, such as hearts, bells, or pieces of fruit, with your hands.

Piggy Puppet

This cute clay puppet will fit you like a glove because you model it right on your own finger.

You will need:
- brown clay
- pick
- bright pink and white paints
- paintbrush
- green fabric
- glue

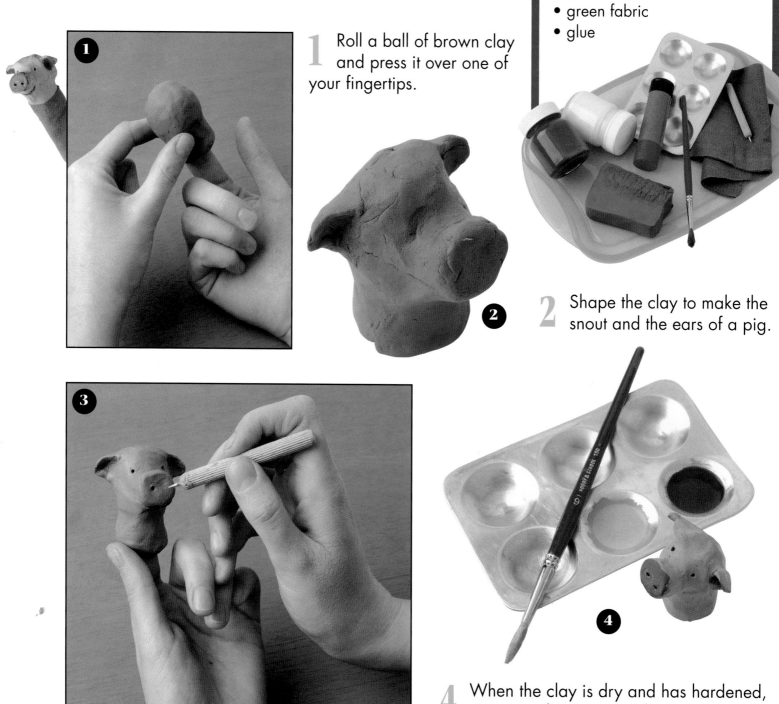

1 Roll a ball of brown clay and press it over one of your fingertips.

2 Shape the clay to make the snout and the ears of a pig.

3 Use a pick to make eyes in the pig's head and small holes in its snout.

4 When the clay is dry and has hardened, paint it with a mixture of bright pink and white paints. After this coat of paint dries, paint the end of the snout and the insides of the ears bright pink.

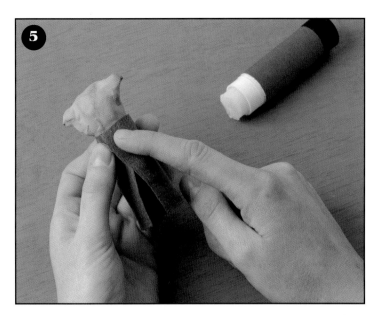

5 Out of green fabric, cut a rectangle that is long enough and wide enough to fit around your finger. Glue the fabric around the outside of the pig's neck.

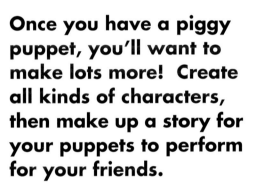

Once you have a piggy puppet, you'll want to make lots more! Create all kinds of characters, then make up a story for your puppets to perform for your friends.

Another Great Idea!
Instead of using fabric around the neck of a puppet to cover your finger, start with more clay and smooth it about halfway down your finger. Then, from the neck down, paint on some decorative designs.

Handprint Tile

Capture the shape of your hand in clay, then decorate it with flashy colors and designs.

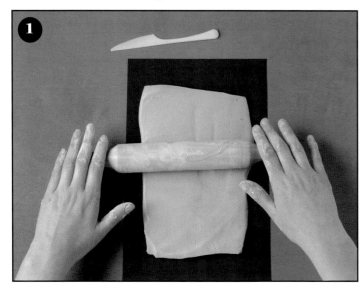

1 Flatten a large lump of white clay with a rolling pin until it is about ¾ inch (2 centimeters) thick. Use a plastic knife to cut the flattened clay into a rectangle. Make the rectangle a little bigger than your hand.

You will need:
- white clay
- rolling pin
- plastic knife
- pick
- wire sculpting loop
- orange, blue, and white paints
- paintbrush

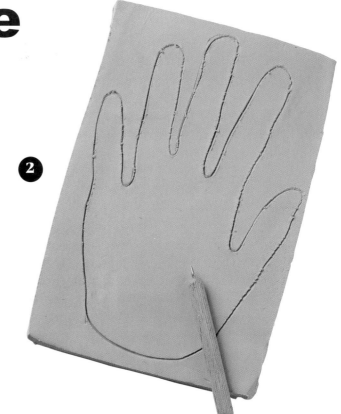

2 Place your hand on the clay and use a pick to make an outline around it. Do not press the pick too hard into the clay.

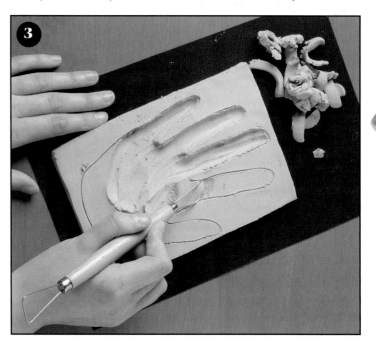

3 Use a wire loop to remove clay from inside the outline. Be sure that you don't make any holes that go all the way through the clay.

4 When the clay is dry and has hardened, paint the handprint orange and the tile around it blue.

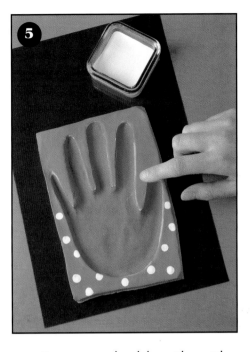

5 Decorate the blue tile with polka dots of white paint. Make the dots with one of your fingertips.

Hang your handprint tile on the wall or set it on a desk or a dresser and use it as a place to keep small objects.

Another Great Idea!
Create more decorative tiles by outlining other shapes or by making drawings in the clay.

Dragon Paperweight

Some big green dragons are just cute and colorful, but this clay heavyweight is useful, too.

You will need:
- white clay
- brown clay
- rolling pin
- plastic knife
- pick
- green paint
- paintbrush

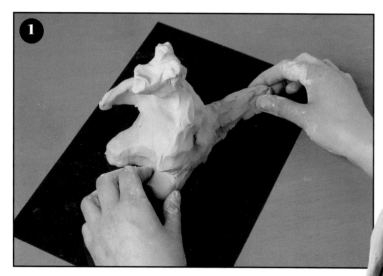

1 Model a large lump of white clay into the shape of a dragon that does not have a belly or a spiky crest down its back.

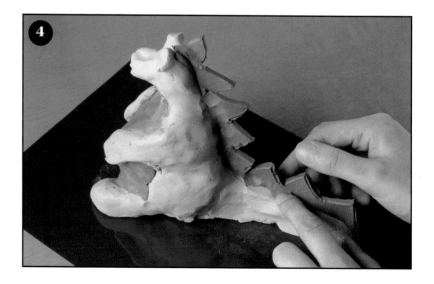

2 Model a lump of brown clay into a round belly. Attach the belly to the dragon by pressing and smoothing the clay with your fingers.

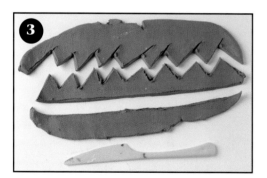

3 Use a rolling pin to flatten another lump of brown clay. With a plastic knife, cut a long row of triangular spikes that will reach from the dragon's head to the end of its tail.

4 Use your fingers to attach the spikes to the dragon's back and tail.

5 Use a pick to make small holes in the clay for eyes and nostrils and to make lines for fingers, toes, and the markings across the dragon's nose and belly.

5

6

6 When the clay is dry and has hardened, paint the white clay green, except for the eyes. Leave the brown clay unpainted.

Perched on papers, your dragon will be a great security guard.

Another Great Idea!
Leave off the spines and the long tail and reshape the head to make a big bear paperweight.

27

Friendly Mug

Make a mug with a protruding nose, rosy cheeks, and a cheery smile. It's almost as much fun as making a new friend.

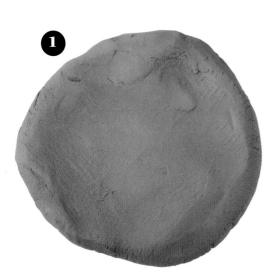

1 Use your hands to roll a lump of brown clay into a ball, then flatten the ball against the top of a table.

2 Roll three pieces of clay into long sausage shapes. Place them, one on top of the other, around the edge of the flattened clay. With your fingers, press and smooth all of the sausages together, both inside and outside.

3 Roll two more pieces of clay into shorter sausage shapes. Press the top and bottom of each sausage onto opposite sides of the mug shape to make handles.

You will need:

- brown clay
- green, orange, white, red, black, and bright pink paints
- paintbrushes
- sponge

4 Roll a small ball of clay and press it onto the outside of the mug halfway between the two handles. Soften the ball of clay with water and model it with your fingers to make it look like a nose.

5 When your clay mug is dry and has hardened, paint the inside and both of the handles green. Paint the outside of the mug orange. Paint the rim of the mug white.

6 After the paint dries, add eyes and a smile. Then use a sponge to dab paint on the end of the nose and to make cheeks. Paint orange polka dots on the mug's handles.

This colorful, smiling mug will brighten your breakfast table, but DO NOT use it for drinking.

Another Great Idea!
Make a decorative mug without a nose. Just paint on stripes, polka dots, or any other colorful pattern or design.

Pencil Sharpener

How can one special pencil keep all of your other pencils sharp? This big clay pencil has a small pencil sharpener hidden inside!

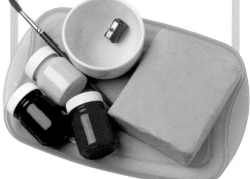

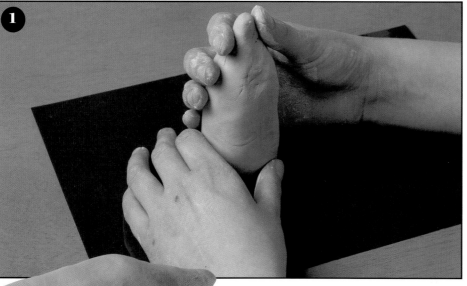

1 Use your hands to roll a lump of white clay into a wide cylinder. Model a point at one end of the cylinder.

2 Take some clay out of the cylinder along the bottom edge. Fit the pencil sharpener in that space. The hole for the pencil should be at the side of the cylinder. The sharpener's blade should be showing on the bottom of the cylinder, so the pencil shavings can fall out.

3 Use a little water and your fingers to smooth the clay.

4 When the clay is dry and has hardened, paint the body of the pencil yellow. Paint only the very top of the pencil's tip black.

5 After the yellow paint dries, paint black lines down the sides of the pencil and paint the bottom of the pencil red.

Now you have a secret way to keep your pencils sharp — and you will never lose your sharpener!

Another Great Idea!
Instead of painting your pencil, use two different colors of clay, then just brush on a coat of varnish.

Glossary

contrasting: looking noticeably different

cylinder: a shape that has curved sides and round, flat ends

dowels: thin, round, smooth sticks or rods made of wood

geometric: having simple shapes, such as squares, circles, rectangles, and triangles, that are based on straight lines

model: (v) to form or shape

nostrils: the openings in a nose

protruding: sticking out

sculpting: shaping or modeling figures the way a sculptor does

seam: the line that forms where two separate parts are joined together

skewers: long, thin, pointed sticks of wood that are normally used to hold meat together while it is roasting

smooth: (v) to gently rub a surface with the hands or fingers to remove roughness

spatter: to scatter or sprinkle, forming a spotted pattern; splatter

triangular: in the shape of a triangle

More Books to Read

Beads 'n' Badges. Handy Crafts (series). Gillian Souter (Gareth Stevens)

Crafts from Modeling Clay. Step by Step (series). Huguette Kirby (Bridgestone Books)

Create Anything with Clay. Sherri Haab and Laura Torres (Klutz Press)

Modeling with Clay. Let's Start (series). Emma Foa (Silver Dolphin)

Play-Doh Animal Fun. Kathy Ross (Millbrook Press)

Web Sites

Family Fun Activities & Crafts: Handprint Soap Dish. family.go.com/crafts/season/ craft/famf0502_craft_soapdish/

Hands on Crafts: Studio 1. Clay Studio. www.handsoncrafts.org/index.htm